Why Me?

Brother Dennis Robert FSC

A Redemptorist Publication

Published by **Redemptorist Publications**
A Registered Charity limited by guarantee.
Registered in England 3261721.

Copyright © 2007 Redemptorist Publications

Cover & Layout: Peena Lad

ISBN-13: 978-0-85231-341-1

Printed by Joseph Ball Limited

Redemptorist
PUBLICATIONS

Alphonsus House Chawton Hampshire GU34 3HQ
Telephone 01420 88222   Fax 01420 88805
rp@rpbooks.co.uk   www.rpbooks.co.uk

Foreword by Fr Timothy Buckley, C.Ss.R.

I first met Brother Dennis Robert in the mid 1950s when I was a boy of ten at St Joseph's College, Beulah Hill, South London. He was the Vocations' Director for the De la Salle Brothers and occasionally would visit our classroom and entertain us in his own inimitable way, hoping to sow the seeds of some future vocations. I recall marching up to his room one lunchtime and telling him that I did not want to become a De la Salle brother but that I was interested in the Redemptorists. He duly sought me out a few days later with a pack of information on the Redemptorists. This was typical of the man: thoughtful, generous and with a meticulous eye for detail.

Even as a child I recognised the warmth of his personality and his wonderfully persuasive powers of communication. Whenever he wanted anything done he would persuade you that this would be the finest venture of its kind, whether it was a Sixth Form panel organised for the Catholic newspaper *The Universe*, or years later, after I was ordained, a "Caring Church Week" designed to transform the spiritual life of the same St Joseph's College. In later years he took thousands of people on pilgrimage, especially to the Holy Land, and there opened the pages of the scriptures for them in a way they would never forget.

It is a special delight for me to have had some part in arranging for this book to be published in his memory. In *Why Me?* he marries his lifelong conviction that each of us is called by God – however much we may on occasion struggle to understand what is going on – with his passion for the word of God. He traces the story of the Old Testament by imagining how some of the key characters chosen by God must have asked themselves why God had chosen them, and brings the story to its conclusion with John the Baptist, the last great prophet of the Old Covenant and the first of the New.

Brother Dennis's many friends will treasure this book. It will remind them of his wit and good humour and his wonderful ability to tell a story with flair and imagination. They will recall too those pregnant pauses after he had stressed some important point by pronouncing every syllable with great precision. For those who did not know Brother Dennis these pages will be a riveting introduction to a man who spent his long life – he died on 19 February 2006 at the age of ninety-four – faithfully proclaiming the Gospel of Jesus.

For anyone who wants a succinct introduction to the Old Testament this book is ideal as it seeks to enter the minds of many of God's faithful servants, so that we can identify with them. It is suitable for people of all ages. It is the kind of book you will find hard to put down.

INTRODUCTION

There must be few men and women who, when they have suffered a great trial, like a protracted illness or the death of a baby, have not said, "But why me?" and, if they are Christians, who have not said, "But why did God do this to me?"

Our Lord spoke words which give the answer to every trial: "Are not two sparrows sold for a penny? And not one of them will fall to the ground without your Father's will. But even the hairs of your head are all numbered. Fear not, therefore; you are of more value than many sparrows" (Matthew 10:29-31).

It takes a great leap of faith to believe this.

This book is the story of twelve of God's friends from the Old Testament and one from the New who took that leap. They were buffeted by trials and tribulations and, in their suffering, eventually found that God their Father did care mightily. But for some it took a long, long time before they found the reassuring answer to "WHY ME?"

One of the most impressive examples for me is that of Joseph of the technicoloured coat. He was hated by his brothers. They put him down a well to die. He was later thrown into an Egyptian prison after a false accusation. It was only after many a sorrowing year that he found out that he was God's cherished instrument, born to transform a nomadic pastoral race into the Jewish nation from which would come the Messiah.

With faith, the theme of this book can be summarised in one word: TRUST.

CONTENTS

ABRAHAM
"Why my Isaac?" laments Sarah

One of the hardest things for many people to accept in the Old Testament is God's order to Abram to sacrifice his only son, Isaac, on Mount Moriah – in what is now Jerusalem – twenty miles from Hebron.

The story starts about 4,000 years ago, where the River Euphrates flows into the Persian Gulf, in a town called Ur. There lived Abram – later to be called Abraham. He was married to Sarai – later to become Sarah – who, tragically, was barren. When he was about seventy-five years old and Sarai was well past sixty Abram was called by God to leave his country and to go to what we now call Canaan.

Twenty-five years went by. One day, at their dwelling in Mamre beside Hebron, Abram saw three young men passing. With traditional eastern hospitality, he invited them into his tent, giving orders to Sarai to bake cakes and to kill a fatted calf. But these were no ordinary young men: they were angels. They told Abram that Sarai would have a son – and nine months later Isaac was born. How Sarai must have rejoiced!

A few years later she saw Abraham take their son to sacrifice him as a burnt offering to God on Mount Moriah – the horror of loss in a horror of flames. How Sarah must have wept! "WHY MY ISAAC?" she must have cried. For a so-called loving God to have ordered a son's death by fire seems callous beyond belief. This is not the God that we know and love. Every fibre of our bodies revolts against the notion. Such thinking does us credit, and yet this revulsion has its origin in this very Abraham and Isaac incident. No one in Abraham's day could have understood our respect for human life.

How to please a god – 4,000 years ago

In Abraham's day human life belonged to the gods. To them no life was sacred. The gods alone were sacred. History books and the Bible are full of this fact. If you wanted to placate a god you offered your greatest possession – and what greater than your firstborn son? Such a sacrifice

9

seemed in those days so natural. It was the done thing. A great need demands a great sacrifice.

Rebuilding Jericho

In the middle of the ninth century, before the Sermon on the Mount and the eight Beatitudes, King Ahab ruled over Israel. He set out to rebuild Jericho which had been totally destroyed by Joshua when the Israelites, after their forty years roaming in the desert under Moses, crossed the River Jordan at Jericho to conquer the Promised Land.

Ahab chose as his architect an expert called Hiel. Hiel wanted to be doubly sure that the new city would be his greatest architectural triumph. Although he knew of the curse that Joshua had put on anyone rebuilding Jericho – he would lose his eldest son and his youngest son – Hiel did the obvious thing: he placated his gods.

He sacrificed his eldest son, Abiram, by making him the foundation stone of the city walls. He sacrificed his youngest son, Segub, making him the cornerstone of the city gates. This was the perfect way to ensure the safety and prosperity of the new Jericho. It would belong to the gods, and they would be with it and would keep it safe for ever. Hiel was a happy man.

Happy gods

When King Ahab of the ten tribes of Israel died in 850 BC King Mesha of neighbouring Moab refused to pay the traditional tribute of 100,000 lambs and as many unshorn rams to King Jehoram, Ahab's successor. Jehoram linked up with King Jehoshaphat of Judah and the King of Edom to punish Mesha.

King Mesha was in dire straits and the only way he could overcome such superior forces was by bribing the gods. He took his firstborn son and successor and sacrificed him on the city walls in full view of his enemies. The Bible says, "And there came great wrath upon Israel; and they withdrew from him and returned to their own land" (2 Kings 3:27).

721 BC is a tragic date for Israel. In that year mighty King Sargon of Assyria conquered the ten tribes of Israel and took the people into captivity. He proceeded to fill the human vacuum with pagans whom he had taken prisoner in other countries. The Bible specifically mentions the Sepharvites who "burned their children in the fire to Adrammelech and Anammelech, the gods of Sepharvaim" (2 Kings 17:31). It was the done thing.

Our God is a jealous God

The cruel captivity of Assyria was God's punishment because the Israelites imitated their pagan neighbours. The Second Book of Kings is most emphatic about this: "And they forsook all the commandments of the Lord their God... and served Baal. And they burned their sons and their daughters as offerings..." (2 Kings 17:16-17). It was under the very walls of Jerusalem, in the Hinnom Valley, that the Jews offered their children to Baal and Moloch.

Wooing the gods

The sacrifice of human life to the gods continued well into the centuries after Christ. Around 2,700 years after Abraham sacrificed, not a child, but a ram on Mount Moriah, the Toltec tribe in what is now Mexico had a great god, Quetzalcoatl, who had to be kept happy and protective by drinking human blood. The greater the need, the greater the flood of human blood needed to win his favours. But Quetzalcoatl failed to save the Toltecs from a still more ferocious tribe, the Aztecs.

The Aztecs had their own gods, Huitzilopochtli and Tezcatlipoca. For good measure Tlacaelel, the Aztec King-Maker, decided to add the Toltec god, Quetzalcoatl, to their litany of gods. There's safety in numbers! Where Mexico City's cathedral now stands, he built a vast temple to this new god. To curry favour with Quetzalcoatl he dedicated the temple with an ocean of blood. Figures differ about the number of victims. History books put the number at between 10,000 and 80,000.

Whatever the number, the method was the same. Relays of priests in teams of four worked day and night in offering victims to the new god. The priests were experts: a belly sliced open with an obsidian knife; the heart ripped out and held up as an offering to Quetzalcoatl and the body thrust down the chute to the animals in the zoo below. The priests reached a speed of fifteen seconds per victim. They stopped only when the last victim had been slaughtered and Quetzalcoatl's thirst satisfied. The Aztecs were so serene: they had triple divine protection.

But note: this massed human sacrifice was not in the days before Christ, but continued until a mere 500 years ago, a time when Henry VIII was on the British throne!

The Life Movement

Abraham, who had worshipped the god Sin in his home city of Ur, would have been dismayed but not astounded to have been ordered by the gods to slay Isaac. This is what the gods did and what the worshippers of the gods expected, and Abraham was a man of his time. He had only the haziest notions of the God who called him, he knew not why, out of the land of Ur.

Abraham was all set to kill Isaac when an angel stopped him. God, said the angel, was satisfied with Abraham's obedience. Seeing a ram caught in the bushes, Abraham took it and offered it as a burnt offering in place of Isaac.

But the day on which God tested the obedience of Abraham by the morals of his age and halted human sacrifice because human life was sacred, that day was the birthday of today's LIFE MOVEMENT some 4,000 years ago.

JOSEPH
Of the technicoloured coat

One tiny monosyllable, uttered by one man, was vital in shaping the history of the Jewish nation – or better, in shaping the history of the world.

Isaac, the son of Abraham and Sarah, had two sons, Esau and Jacob, the more outstanding being Jacob. Jacob was more prolific than his father: he produced twelve sons, the greatest and most beloved being Joseph. Joseph was an extraordinary teenager. He had repeated visions of his own greatness. He was his father's favourite son – the son of his old age. Jacob dressed him in a coat, beautifully and colourfully embroidered – and he has passed into history as Joseph of the technicoloured coat.

Because Joseph was so special to Jacob, his brothers brooded over this preferential treatment, and that brooding turned into hatred. They hated him still more vehemently when he began to tell them of his visions. One vision cut them to the quick. He explained that, in his dream, all of them were binding sheaves in the corn field. His own sheaf stood erect and theirs bowed and did reverence to his. He shared another dream with his brothers, telling how the moon and eleven stars did reverence to him, the sun. Indeed, Joseph was an extraordinary teenager. But, to put it mildly, his brothers were not impressed.

The teenage slave
Joseph was sixteen years old when his father sent him on an errand. His brothers were tending sheep at Shechem, some fifty miles from Hebron. He was to check how his brothers were faring and to report back.

It was going to be many years before he could report back! His baneful brothers saw him coming from afar and decided to kill him and to throw his body down a well. They would explain to their father that Joseph had been killed by a wild animal and they would produce his blood-stained coat as evidence. They did indeed throw Joseph down a deep, dry well, but, as they ate their meal, a company of Ishmaelites passed by on their way to Egypt with their spices, balm and myrrh for sale. Joseph's brothers had second thoughts. They dragged Joseph out of the well, and sold him to the Ishmaelites for blood money – twenty pieces of silver. Now the merchants had Joseph, a slave, for sale too, and they took him to Egypt. Surely Joseph in his bewilderment must have asked God, "WHY ME?"

A woman's wiles

Joseph must have been a handsome youth – a sun among stars – with a charism which radiated. It was the captain of Pharaoh's guard, Potiphar, who bought him, and a man of his station wanted only the best. Because Joseph was beautiful in face and form, Potiphar's wife desired him, wooed him, enticed him, harassed him, using all her wiles to ensnare him. But Joseph said, "NO" to her evil desires.

To her husband, on his return home, she accused Joseph of attempted rape. Potiphar, in a towering rage, threw Joseph into prison. Once again Joseph must surely have asked his God, "WHY ME?" In the words of the Bible, "But the Lord was with Joseph and showed him steadfast love…" (Genesis 39:21).

Prison

The rest of the story has gone down into history. Joseph was joined in prison by the King of Egypt's butler and baker who had offended their master. Both baker and butler had a different inexplicable dream. Joseph interpreted the dreams for them: the butler was to be released in three days, but the baker would be beheaded in three days. And the dreams came true.

Later, the Pharaoh himself had two inexplicable dreams – of seven fat and seven lean cows and then of seven ears of ripe corn and seven of shrivelled corn. (Both of these stories make fascinating reading in Genesis 40 to 41.) When none of Pharaoh's magicians could explain the dreams, the butler remembered Joseph's gift of interpretation and told Pharaoh about a young Hebrew who could explain dreams. Pharaoh immediately summoned Joseph from prison. Joseph did indeed explain Pharaoh's dream. There were to be seven years of plenty and seven years of famine. Joseph suggested that Pharaoh should appoint a wise man to store grain in the years of plenty so as to have food for the seven years of famine. Joseph himself was appointed to this role and was made governor of all Egypt, second only to the king.

If Joseph had said, "YES"

If Joseph had said, "YES" to Potiphar's wife's evil desires, how would God have followed through with his plan for the Messiah and for our redemption?

Joseph was thirty years old when Pharaoh took the royal seal from his own finger and put it on Joseph's and gave him a royal chariot and a guard of honour. For a score of years Joseph had been querying God's wisdom and caring. For a score of years he had been saying to God, "WHY ME?" At thirty he was beginning to get a glimmering of God's goodness and of God's plan for the race of Israel and indeed for the human race.

Without the terrible tragedies that Joseph had had to endure there would have been no comely Joseph to have been wrongfully accused by Potiphar's wife and thrown into prison. There would have been no Joseph to interpret the butler's and the baker's dreams. There would have been no Joseph to be summoned to interpret Pharaoh's dream. Joseph would not have become Egypt's leading statesman: his family would not have been invited by Pharaoh to make their home in Egypt, and these nomadic, pastoral people would not have achieved the nationhood which they did in the years between Joseph's death and the birth of Moses.

The sequel is self-evident. There would have been no mass immigration of Jews into the fair land of Goshen, no Egyptian jealousy and fear, no mass destruction of the Jewish firstborn sons, and later of the

Egyptians' firstborn sons. There would have been no Prince Moses to lead this new nation to the Promised Land. There would have been no Jesse, no King Saul, and therefore no King David, no genealogy leading through King David to the Bethlehemite Joseph of Nazareth, no marriage of Mary and Joseph.

One small word

Little could Joseph have known, when he resolutely said NO to evil, that that tiny monosyllable would shape the history of the world. One tiny monosyllable ushered in a new epoch, opening wide the door to the Messiah. It took Joseph many painful years to know the answer to his plaintive teenage question:

"Why ME?"

We may never know the answer to some of the perplexing or harrowing happenings which we ourselves may have to suffer. But one thing is certain: we shall spend eternity thanking God for his goodness and his fatherly love which will always be his answer to our own:

"But why ME?"

MOSES
"Why me?" pleads Moses

If ever there was a person who knew without a shadow of doubt that he was totally unfitted for the mission God was giving him, that person was Moses. If ever there was a person who had every right to say to God, "But why me?" that person was definitely Moses.

It was many years since Joseph of the technicoloured coat had ruled Egypt. It was many years since Pharaoh had welcomed the nomadic Israelites into Egypt and set them up in the land of Goshen. Great had been their welcome. Pharaoh had said to Joseph, "Your father and your brothers have come to you. The land of Egypt is before you; settle your father and your brothers in the best of the land..." (Genesis 47:5-6).

Since that initial period of peace the Israelites had become a potential menace to the Egyptians because of their expanding population. They were little by little degraded and now in the fourteenth century before Christ they were suffering all the agonies of slavery in Egypt, living under the lash of many a foreman in many a brickyard and many a quarry.

Bricks unending
There was no lack of such work. The Pharaohs were great builders. The Giza Khufu pyramid near Cairo, for instance, was so vast that St Peter's Basilica and the cathedrals of Florence, Milan, St Paul's and Westminster Abbey could all be grouped within its area. It is estimated that 2,300,000 blocks of stone, each weighing around two and a half tons, were needed for this pyramid, which took 100,000 men twenty years to build. Pharaohs thought big, so there was no lack of work for the tens of thousands of brick-makers and quarry workers!

It was in this setting that Moses, Jewish by birth and Egyptian by adoption, had committed the unpardonable: to protect a Jewish slave he had killed an Egyptian foreman. It was unpardonable because even to strike a taskmaster endangered the whole slave system of Egypt. Even rank or title could not remain unpunished, and so, to escape the death sentence, Prince Moses fled to the Midianite country. He sought refuge with the wise priest, Jethro, marrying his daughter and peacefully tending the sheep.

It was here that God awaited him. Here God appeared in the burning bush to the fugitive Moses on Mount Horeb and commissioned him to free the Israelites from their bondage. God told the awestruck Moses that he was to return to Egypt, to gather the elders of Israel together and to tell them that God had appeared to him and given him a mission. That mission was to go to the Pharaoh and tell him he was to let the Israelites go into the wilderness to offer sacrifice to the Lord.

Was Moses exhilarated at being chosen for such a sublime mission? No way. He protested his inability. He pointed out to God what God ought to have known – that he was totally unfit for the task: "Oh, my Lord, I am not eloquent... but I am slow of speech and of tongue" (Exodus 4:10). God sought to reassure a diffident Moses. He promised that he, the Lord, would help him to speak and would tell him exactly what he had to say to Pharaoh. Even this failed to reassure Moses who again protested his inability: "Oh, my Lord, send, I pray, some other person" (Exodus 4:13).

Moses was the perfect patient for the psychiatrist's couch! He had such a massive inferiority complex that he continued to try to wriggle out of his mission until at last "the anger of the Lord was kindled against Moses..." (Exodus 4:14). But finally it was God who gave in! He produced a compromise: "Is there not Aaron, your brother, the Levite? I know that he can speak well... He shall speak for you to the people; and he shall be a mouth for you, and you shall be to him as God" (Exodus 4:14, 16) So when Moses and Aaron summoned the elders, it was Aaron who spoke to them. He needed all his eloquence: he had to convince these cowed slaves that they had to launch a crusade, to turn on their all-powerful masters, and to accept this vision of freedom as a fact. Aaron succeeded magnificently while Moses stood ineptly by!

A mighty Pharaoh

An additional reason for Moses' fear was that he knew this Pharaoh only too well. This Pharaoh, according to many historians, was Rameses the Second, at whose court Moses would have been prince. This Rameses stands out as one of the greatest of the great Pharaohs. He was god-king of Egypt. He was an outstanding warrior. Prince Moses may well have been at his side in one of his frequent campaigns against the Hittites. Rameses was a great builder and Prince Moses might well have frequently escorted him when they passed the Israelites slaving at their brick-making.

Egypt was peopled with colossal statues of Rameses. His temples and palaces were monumental, glowing with grandiose scenes of his victories depicted in brilliant colours, like the battle scenes exhibited in the British Museum. One recalls the almost impossible task undertaken in the 1960s merely to move one of Rameses' gigantic temples – the Abu Simbel – to safety from Nile waters rising from behind the Aswan High Dam.

The long reign of Rameses – from 1304 to 1237 BC – was famous for its efflorescence in sculptures, ceramics and ornate furnishings of gold, silver and jewellery. After all, we have, so to speak, glimpsed the splendour of Rameses the Second in the treasures of Tutankhamen which dazzled the art world in the 1920s. Tutankhamen preceded Rameses by only half a century. And in that intervening half-century Rameses had learned to better Tutankhamen's best.

This was the mighty Pharaoh whom Moses and Aaron had to confront: a Pharaoh from whom Prince Moses had fled, with the death penalty hanging over him. How Moses must have quailed at the mere thought. Not unlikely it was the overpowering personality of Pharaoh Rameses which had caused an adopted Prince Moses to develop so shattering an inferiority complex and a nervous stutter of which he was so painfully aware.

Pharaoh rebuffed Moses and Aaron, berating them for their laziness, and as punishment ordered the overseers to pressurise their people into making the same number of bricks, but with one difference. In future they were not to be provided with straw but were to find their own.

Moses fails

So Moses, in spite of the help of an eloquent Aaron, failed totally. He had as much as told God that he'd fail. God really ought to have known better than to choose so helpless a helper. Worse, Moses had incurred the bitter anger of the Israelites: "The Lord look upon you and judge, because you have made us offensive in the sight of Pharaoh and his servants, and have put a sword in their hand to kill us" (Exodus 5:21).

And Moses turned to God, almost reproaching him: "Why didst thou ever send me? For since I came to Pharaoh to speak in thy name, he has done evil to this people, and thou hast not delivered thy people at all" (Exodus 5:22-23). It was in vain that God reaffirmed his promise to give the Israelites a land flowing with milk and honey. When Moses told this to the elders of Israel they snubbed him. In the words of the Bible, "they did not listen to Moses, because of their broken spirit and their cruel bondage" (Exodus 6:9).

But there was no escape route for Moses. God confirmed a reluctant Moses in his mission and again ordered him to order Pharaoh to let his people go. And again Moses hung back and pleaded with God: that since the sons of Israel had not listened to him, why should Pharaoh do so?

So God gave Moses a most powerful weapon – the ten plagues inflicted on the Egyptians. The Nile was turned into blood; the country was invaded by frogs and gnats and swarms of flies, followed by a sirocco wind bringing locusts which darkened the skies, covered the whole face of the ground and devoured what was left of the crop. Egypt was then assailed by a most grievous plague, followed by ulcers and boils, followed by thunder and fire, and an all-destroying hail which ruined whatever harvest the locusts had not devoured; and then a total darkness covered all Egypt except Goshen, the land of the Israelites.

God's final weapon was the death of the firstborn of every Egyptian man or beast. The mighty Pharaoh was crushed.

A short-lived triumph

As for Moses, his trials surely were over. Henceforth he would be able to bask in the unstinted admiration and total adulation of his people: he had set God's people free. But the adulation did not last long. Pharaoh had a change of heart and he and his army followed them into the desert. The Israelites found themselves caught between charging chariots and the sea. They turned on Moses: "What have you done to us, in bringing us out of Egypt?... For it would have been better for us to serve the Egyptians than to die in the wilderness" (Exodus 14:11-12).

But the Lord came to the help of Moses. The waters of the Red Sea stopped flowing, allowing the Israelites to cross safely. When the Egyptian army was crossing in pursuit of the Israelites the waters flowed again and engulfed the Egyptian army. Fortunately, after their deliverance from the Egyptians drowned in the Red Sea, the people "believed in the Lord and in his servant Moses" (Exodus 14:31). Once again it was a period of admiration and adulation! "Then Miriam, the prophetess, the sister of Aaron, took a timbrel in her hand; and all the women went out after her with timbrels and dancing. And Miriam sang to them:
> 'Sing to the Lord, for he has triumphed gloriously;
> the horse and his rider he has thrown into the sea'"
> (Exodus 15:20-21).

Indeed, there was no god like their God, and no hero like their Moses.

Groans and grumbles

But not for long. When they marched through the wilderness of Shur to Marah with its bitter waters, once again "the people murmured against Moses, saying, 'What shall we drink?'" (Exodus 15:24). Wherever he went, Moses found the elders moaning beside their tents: "Would that we had died by the hand of the Lord in the land of Egypt, when we sat by the fleshpots and ate bread to the full" (Exodus 16:3).

Loud too were their mutterings at Rephidim where they clamoured for water, and once again they turned against Moses and growled, "Give us water to drink" (Exodus 17:2). Tragic Moses. To the Israelites he pleaded, "Why do you find fault with me?" (Exodus 17:2) and to the Lord he cried, "They are almost ready to stone me" (Exodus 17:4).

Family feud

Even Moses' family turned against him. Aaron, his own brother, led the people in their desire for man-made gods, himself melting down golden jewellery to make a golden calf. He himself, while Moses was conversing with the Lord and receiving the Ten Commandments on Mount Sinai, erected an altar and offered burnt sacrifices to the golden calf. The nephews of Moses, Nadab and Abihu, puffed up with jealous pride, tried to rival him in his role of intercessor with God, sacrilegiously burning unhallowed fire in the tabernacle.

His sister and brother, Miriam and Aaron, began a painful family feud, resenting the wife Moses had chosen. Further, they tried to usurp or at least to share his authority. They murmured, "Has the Lord indeed spoken only through Moses? Has he not spoken through us also?" (Numbers 12:2). "And the anger of the Lord was kindled against them, and... behold, Miriam was leprous, as white as snow" (Numbers 12:9-10).

And wherever he passed beside the tents Moses was forever surrounded by folk venting their spleen, loud with accusation and cursing him for their hard lot: "O that we had meat to eat! We remember the fish we ate in Egypt for nothing, the cucumbers, the melons, the leeks, the onions, and the garlic; but now our strength is dried up, and there is nothing at all but this manna to look at" (Numbers 11:4-6).

Moses was racked with woe at his recurring failure: "I am not able to carry all this people alone, the burden is too heavy for me. If thou wilt deal thus with me, kill me at once, if I find favour in thy sight, that I may not see my wretchedness" (Numbers 11:14-15). And God sent quails.

Throughout the time the Israelites were in the desert Moses had to bear with whimpering, mutterings, grumblings, complaints and revolt. He still battled on, even to the bitter end. When the Israelites were actually in sight of the Promised Land, the messengers Moses had sent to spy it out returned from Canaan, and most of them betrayed him. They lied: "The land, through which we have gone, to spy it out, is a land that devours its inhabitants; and all the people that we saw in it are men of great stature... and we seemed to ourselves like grasshoppers, and so we seemed to them" (Numbers 13:32-33).

Open revolt

So once again Moses was at the receiving end of the Israelites' rage: "Then all the congregation raised a loud cry; and the people wept that night. And all the people of Israel murmured against Moses and Aaron..." (Numbers 14:1-2). That night Moses must surely have retired to his tent, and with his head cradled in his hands he must have cried to God:

"Why ME?"

But in some Israelites' tents there was more than rage: there was revolt. Because of the fear inspired by the lying messengers there was a movement to depose Moses as leader, and to name a new leader to take them all back to Egypt! When two of the messengers, Caleb and Joshua, protested that the people had been deceived, affirming that the land was ready to fall into their hands, the multitude cried out to stone them.

Then there was open revolt by 250 of the leading elders under the banner of Korah, Dathan and Abiram. They confronted Moses and Aaron: "You have gone too far! For all the congregation are holy, every one of them, and the Lord is among them; why then do you exalt yourselves above the assembly of the Lord?" (Numbers 16:3). Revolt followed revolt, followed revolt. The people were so threatening that Moses and Aaron had to take refuge in the sacred tabernacle. Their very lives were in danger.

At Kadesh, in the desert of Zin, the mood of the people once again became ugly: "Would that we had died when our brethren died before the Lord! Why have you brought the assembly of the Lord into this wilderness, that we should die here, both we and our cattle? And why have you made us come up out of Egypt, to bring us to this evil place? It is no place for grain, or figs, or vines, or pomegranates; and there is no water to drink" (Numbers 20:3-5). The place was named the Waters of Rebellion.

For forty years, grumbling and bickering against Moses was the order of the day. At Edom God punished those snarling against him and Moses with a plague of poisonous serpents; Korah and his 250 rebels met God's punishment when the earth opened and swallowed them up; at Sinai there was the frightening Place of Burning.

But still these Israelites wouldn't learn. Throughout their trek through the desert rebels were forever saying to Moses:

"Why YOU?"

And throughout all that time their agonising, tongue-tied leader was forever saying to God:

"Why ME?"

Every Jew praying today at the Wailing Wall – or Western Wall – knows, and is for ever grateful for, the answer. For nearly three and a half millennia they have been thanking God that Moses had the courage to say "YES" to Yahweh. The "YES" of Moses allowed a nation, born in Egypt, to reach maturity.

Further, God needed a messenger to proclaim to nations steeped in the worship of multiple gods, the existence and the nature of the one, true God. God needed a messenger to guide humankind in leading a life worthy of this one, true God – which is through the Ten Commandments, given to Moses on Mount Sinai. That is why God called Moses, and, thank God, God's messenger did not let God down.

DEBORAH
Who fights the impossible fight... and wins

When the Jews entered Egypt they had been pastoral tribes, simple, nomadic wanderers. When they left Egypt with Moses around 400 years later they emerged as a nation. Moses led this nation to the frontier of the Promised Land, and Joshua conquered that Promised Land. Game, set and match! But not quite. Joshua divided the conquered country among the twelve tribes, and this very division carried with it seeds of destruction.

There was no national army, no central administration, and no national successor to Joshua. Each tribe regained its independent authority and jealously guarded it. Unity became fragmentation. The new nation returned to its tribal roots. But they divided at their peril. In the second half of the thirteenth century the sea-based Philistines were foraging inland and the Midianites produced their new weapon – the domesticated camel for long-range raids. Moreover, the five Canaanite nations of the north, centred around Hazor, were determined to stage a comeback from their defeat by Joshua. There was no question of how to "Divide and Conquer". The enemy didn't have to. The Israelites were already divided, ready to be conquered.

Baal and Ashtoreth

A still greater problem faced them: intermarriage. As the Israelites were digging themselves into their conquered territory, they wooed and wed into a conquered people who brought their own gods to the Lord's altar. The Canaanite divinities, like Baal and Ashtoreth, were venerated side by side with the Lord. Tragically, they often displaced the Lord.

Baal was a galaxy of gods. Every spot had its fertility deity, a supernatural power alive in every tree, every babbling brook, every bubbling spring. This became nature worship, leading on to disgusting sensuality. Ashtoreth (who was called Ishtar by the Assyrians and Astarte by the Greeks) was Baal's female companion. She was the goddess of fertility; and fertility developed into untrammelled sexuality and bestiality. Not one of her temples was without a regiment of prostitutes to pander to the obscene desires of her lecherous devotees. Lust was canonised.

Recurring decimals

These are the gods the Jews embraced in place of their Lord. The tragedy for the Jews was that – as had already happened in their forty years in the desert – they could never learn their lesson. From the time when they set up the golden calf in the desert, they hankered after these Baals and Ashtoreths. The Lord was ousted and replaced by the gods of the Canaanites, the Hittites, the Hivites and the Jebusites.

The people of Israel "forsook the Lord, the God of their fathers, who had brought them out of the land of Egypt; they went after other gods, from among the gods of the peoples who were round about them, and bowed down to them; and they provoked the Lord to anger" (Judges 2:12). It became recurring decimals.

The Israelites challenged the Lord's anger. So God left them at the mercy of Cushan-Rishathaim, King of Mesopotamia, who for eight years became their master, and not a merciful master. The Israelites cried out to God in their agony and he sent them a champion, Othniel, to rescue them. They enjoyed forty years of peace. But unfortunately the Israelites had a short memory. Once again they defied the Lord. The Lord's avenger was King Eglon of Moab who defeated them and held them in bondage for eighteen years.

In their suffering the Israelites again cried out to God. The story of how left-handed Ehud killed the gross and pampered King Eglon and again freed the Israelites is a story in its own right. It's told in the Book of Judges 3:15-30 and makes powerful reading. Ehud's victory gave the Israelites eighty years of peace, by the end of which time the Lord had again been eclipsed by foreign gods, and so the Lord put them at the mercy of Jabin, the Canaanite king who ruled in Hazor. No wonder that Israel cried out once again to the Lord! The wonder is that the Lord heard them. But he did. This time he sent a wonder-woman to rescue them.

The Judges

Because at this time there was no national authority, it was the custom for each tribe to elect a leader to promote peace and to dispense judgement. This person was called a Judge. One thinks immediately of Samson, Gideon, Othniel and Jephthah, the man who never smiled.

There was no united action among the twelve tribes. If the Philistines attacked one tribe the other eleven holed themselves in, hoping that their turn would not come. It was only when the Ark of the Covenant was captured by the Philistines that the twelve tribes realised that like other victorious nations they needed a king to forge them into a nation.

The Northern League

Another event previous to this had confirmed the conviction that Israel needed a king. This happened when the five northern nations, under the leadership of King Jabin of Hazor, made a concerted attack on Israel. This attack on Israel's national independence was perhaps the most perilous that Israel had had to repulse. Twenty years before, the Canaanites had subjugated Israel and held them in cruel bondage. Up to then King Jabin had wanted their money. Now he wanted their land.

Judge Deborah was inspired to solve all Israel's problems in one fell swoop. She had to rid the country of King Jabin. He was the most powerful king of the north and he had rallied round him four other local kings to destroy Israel utterly. His plan was simple. Once again it was "Divide and Conquer". With a pincer movement he planned to seize the valley of Jezreel and so cut off northern Israel from the south and gobble each one in turn. The Commander-in-Chief of the five nations was Sisera. His terrible weapon was 900 iron-scythed chariots with sharp knives at their wheels.

Deborah, Barak and God

Deborah summoned an outstanding Israelite soldier, Barak, and gave him his orders. He was to muster 10,000 warriors and lead them to mastery over Jabin and his allies. "Why ME?" Barak must have pleaded. He knew that Deborah was asking the impossible. The Canaanites and the Philistines had the monopoly of iron chariots and iron weapons. The Israelites were, by comparison, militarily naked. But sensing how close Deborah was to God, Barak said, "If you will go with me, I will go; but if you will not go with me, I will not go" (Judges 4:8). Deborah had the answer. She would go with Barak because she knew for certain that God would go with her. And God did.

Down from Mount Tabor swept Barak and his 10,000 men into the plain of Jezreel – only too aware that they were totally powerless against 900 scythe-mounted chariots. And then Deborah's God came into the battle. The Canaanites' shouts of certain victory became screams of fear. The God of Israel opened the floodgates of the skies and torrential rain swept the plain. The swollen River Kishon burst its banks. The heavy iron chariots sank into the soft soil. The fleeing charioteers were slaughtered to the last man.

Sisera, taking refuge and sleeping in the apparently safe tent of Heber the Kenite, never woke up. Jael, Heber's wife, soothed Sisera to sleep and then drove a tent-peg through his brain into the ground below, and he passed from the numbness of sleep to the numbness of death.

Jabin was crushed, and Deborah sang the song of triumph which has passed down into the literature of the world's finest exultant songs: "Hear, O kings; give ear, O princes; to the Lord I will sing, I will make melody to the Lord, the God of Israel... So perish all thine enemies, O Lord! But thy friends be like the sun as he rises in his might" (Judges 5:3-31).

A new chapter had been written in the annals of God's people: "If you will go with me, I will go; but if you will not go with me, I will not go" (Judges 4:8). It was a chapter of total trust. And no good Jew has ever forgotten it.

JEPHTHAH
Whose heroic teenage daughter didn't say, "Why me?"

Had she lived today, she would probably have ended up running an eminently successful psychiatric clinic in this age when so many of the nation are making for the psychiatric couch, and when the media are pouring out more and more facts (and fancies) on stress, strain and heart failure. I say that she would have run an eminently successful clinic because this young girl – for young girl she was – had the total answer to stress, strain and mental pain.

We don't know her name, but we do know the name of her father and his unfortunate background. He was Jephthah, with his family home in Gilead, east of Jordan. He lived in the time of the Judges, just after Joshua's conquest of the Promised Land.

The Judges

Although Joshua had conquered the Promised Land, his successors had no easy time consolidating their gains. It is obvious that the vanquished strove mightily to regain their lost territory. A succession of leaders, called Judges, had held off the attacks of the enemy. These Judges were mostly good, strong men, firm in their faith, like Samson and Gideon. One Judge, Tola, led the Israelites for twenty-three years. Jair was their Judge for twenty-two years. But when Jair died there was no worthy champion to succeed him.

Without God-centred leadership, the people fell to worshipping the Baals, the Ashtoreths, the gods of Syria, the gods of Sidon, the gods of Moab, the gods of the Ammonites and the gods of the Philistines. "And the anger of the Lord was kindled against Israel, and he sold them into the hand of the Philistines and into the hand of the Ammonites, and they crushed and oppressed the children of Israel..." (Judges 10:7-8). The children of Israel got the message. They repented and put away the foreign gods. And then they looked round for a human saviour.

The bandit

They needed a saviour because one of the most powerful of the vanquished nations was Ammon. Against the Ammonites, the Israelites were powerless because leaderless. They found their saviour in Jephthah of Gilead, but to invite him they had to humble themselves. Jephthah has been called "the man who never smiled". He had little enough to smile about. His father begot him from a harlot, and his illegitimacy rankled. He had brothers, but these were legitimate. As the family grew up his brothers turned against him, denied him a share of the inheritance and made life unbearable; so he fled his home. He became a bandit. He gathered around him a company of penniless robbers in the land of Tob, a dozen miles south of the Sea of Galilee.

The Ammonites were harrying the land of Gilead, and the Israelites could not drive them away. So great was Jephthah's warrior fame that a delegation from Gilead tracked him down and begged him to free them from the Ammonites. In return, they offered to make him absolute ruler. Jephthah and his freebooters accepted the challenge. To avoid bloodshed he sent messengers to try to settle the strife peacefully. He was a consummate and patient negotiator. The Ammonites did not share his wisdom: they spurned the messengers. It was war. Jephthah knew that it would be a dangerous war, with victory in the balance. He knew he needed God on his side.

The vow

To woo the Lord, Jephthah made a vow in the way that pagans made vows to their own puny gods. He promised to sacrifice the first living creature that came out of his home if he returned victorious. God would have, as thanksgiving, a burnt offering. Victorious he was. He drove the Ammonites out of twenty cities; he brought them to the dust, and returned home in triumph.

Teenage loyalty

The triumph was short-lived. He had only one child, a daughter whom he dearly loved. It was she who came out of the house, dancing to timbrels, to welcome her victorious father home. A broken man, he told her of his vow.

And now comes the most incredible part of the story. Her respect for God and for a promise made to God was so great that it was she who consoled her father: "My father, if you have opened your mouth to the Lord, do to me according to what has gone forth from your mouth, now that the Lord has avenged you on your enemies, on the Ammonites" (Judges 11:36).

It is not possible to tell the sequel more simply than in the very words of the Bible: "And she said to her father, 'Let this thing be done for me; let me alone two months, that I may go and wander on the mountains, and bewail my virginity, I and my companions.' And he said, 'Go'" (Judges 11:37-38). So she went away with her companions that were her friends and fellows to weep a maiden's tears.

And when the two months were over, she came back to her father. Shattered, he nevertheless fulfilled his promise and she died unwed. That is why the custom grew up in Israel which has been kept ever afterwards, that for four days in every year the maidens of Israel should gather and make lament for the daughter of Jephthah the Gileadite. And lamentation was surely admiration.

Surely, too, this maiden, whose name we do not know, was God's teenage triumph, to stand as an inspiration for all teenagers for all time.

RUTH
"Why am I, an alien woman, so honoured?"
asks Ruth

The Bible gives us, with quiet strength, a condemnation of apartheid 3,000 years ago.

In the time of the Judges there was a famine in Bethlehem and a married man, Elimelech, took his wife, Naomi, and his two sons into Moabite country. Both sons, Mahlon and Chilion, married Moabite wives called Orpah and Ruth. Elimelech died and Naomi was left a widow; but her love of her sons outstripped the love of her country, and she remained in this foreign land with her sons.

After ten years these in turn died and so, widowed and childless, she decided to return to Bethlehem. Orpah and Ruth set out with her. When she reached the town boundary she turned to her daughters-in-law and told them to go back to their kith and kin. After some half-hearted protests Orpah kissed Naomi and reluctantly and tearfully returned home.

Orpah was in no way uncaring. She had her feet set firmly on the ground. She knew how the Jews loathed the inhabitants of Moab. The Moabites had refused the Jews permission to pass through their country as the refugees from Egypt trekked, with Moses, towards the Promised Land. This the Jews had never forgotten nor forgiven. Further, marriage was every woman's dream. To be a mother, and especially the mother of a son, was the highest honour open to an eastern woman. The word Orpah means gazelle – small, swift, graceful – and she wisely decided to find love in Moab rather than suffer an arranged marriage or to live, a hated spinster, in a foreign land.

"Your God shall be my God"
Not so Ruth. She stubbornly refused to leave her mother-in-law: "Entreat me not to leave you or to return from following you; for where you go I will go, and where you lodge I will lodge; your people shall be

my people, and your God my God; where you die I will die, and there will I be buried" (Ruth 1:16-17). In the face of such resolution, Naomi gave up; and so, together, they set out for Bethlehem.

Orpah was wise. Ruth was caring. Out of loyalty to her dead husband's family, Ruth chose to go into a foreign land where she would be a despised stranger; worse, a hated stranger – because she worshipped Moabite gods. Her decision and her self-sacrifice were heroic.

And so Jewish-born Naomi and Moabite-born Ruth returned to Bethlehem when the farmers were beginning to cut the barley. It was a strict tradition that the poor were allowed to gather the leavings when the harvesters had passed and, to support her mother-in-law and herself, Ruth went gleaning after the reapers. Providentially – since nothing happens by chance – the field in which Ruth gleaned belonged to Elimelech's kinsman, Boaz, a man of great wealth and influence, and a bachelor.

Boaz came over to see the reapers. He was impressed by this maiden and, having heard her story, was struck by her devotedness to her Jewish mother-in-law. He renewed the permission for Ruth to continue gleaning. He actually quietly suggested to his reapers that they should discreetly leave corn behind for Ruth to gather. He made a further concession for her: "And when you are thirsty, go to the vessels and drink what the young men have drawn" (Ruth 2:9). Then came Ruth's "Why me?" and her words to Boaz were significant: "Why have I found favour in your eyes, that you should take notice of me, when I am a foreigner?" (Ruth 2:10). She knew well that she did not belong. But subsequent events proved her wrong.

To cut a long romantic story short, Naomi schemed a marriage for Ruth. Boaz wedded and bedded Ruth, and the child that was born from this mixed marriage was called Obed. Obed had a son called Jesse, and Jesse was the father of David. Yes, of King David, the brightest gem in the crown of Israel. (A Jesse painting, window or sculpture illustrates the genealogy of Our Lord. Jesse, the grandson of Ruth and Boaz, and the father of King David, was an ancestor of Jesus. So it is said that

Jesus came from the ROOT or the TREE OF JESSE. Jesse is always depicted lying down, with a tree growing from his belly. In some illustrations, from the stem of the tree grow branches, each with a figure of an ancestor of Jesus, for example, David with a harp, Solomon with a sword. The topmost branch might have the whole history of the birth of Jesus – Mary with the newborn babe, St Joseph, the shepherds, sheep and the sheepdog, the wise men, animals and flying angels.)

450 years on
Turn on the pages of history from King David to around 550 BC. The Jews were in bondage in Babylon under Cyrus of Persia. Cyrus deservedly became known as Cyrus the Great. His grandfather had ordered him to be killed at birth. A shepherd saved him. Soon, with a swift and brilliant rise to power, Cyrus was at the head of the Persians. He banished his cruel grandfather. He conquered King Croesus of Lydia, King Amasis of Egypt and King Nabonidus of Babylon. In doing so he became master of the greatest empire ever seen. He was an enlightened and tolerant conqueror. He allowed the cherished local gods of the nations he had conquered to be set up again. In 538 BC he published an edict allowing those Jews who wished to do so to return to Jerusalem. (This edict has been found by archaeologists at Ecbatana in today's Iran, and is now in the British Museum.)

42,360 Jews, with 7,337 servants and maids, returned to Jerusalem and found it desolate. Nehemiah, the king's cup-bearer, led one group back. The Jews who had not been taken to Babylon were hostile as he and his followers set about rebuilding the walls of Jerusalem, working with a trowel in one hand and a protective spear in the other.

In 459 BC Ezra the scribe led another group of Jews the 800 miles back to the Promised Land. And in this Promised Land he found the abomination of desolation. Priests and the common folk who had been left behind in Jerusalem at the time of the Babylonian captivity had contaminated the sacred stock of Israel by intermarriage with the abominable foreigners imported by Nebuchadnezzar, foreigners who had brought their own gods with them. This racial impurity had to be ended. Ezra and the clan chiefs summoned everyone, family by family, man by man, and checked their marriage record. Within three months, all the husbands of foreign wives had passed before them.

A pure-blooded nation
Priests who could not find a written record of their ancestry were expelled from the priesthood. All others – Levites, Temple singers, Temple door-keepers and common folk – had to make a vow to drive away their abominable foreign wives and their detestable children. Their children! Nehemiah found that some of these, so unlike true Jews, spoke partly in the Philistine dialect. He fumed that they would use the speech first of one race and then of another. He put a curse on the fathers of such children; he came to blows with them and plucked the hair from their heads.

On the twenty-fourth day of the month, the whole race of Israel assembled. This was the first Jewish Knesset (Parliament). They pledged themselves to the Torah – that is, the entire body of Jewish teachings; they severed themselves publicly and totally from these alien people. And when this was done, the nation was once again a pure, true blue-blooded nation. This was apartheid at its most quintessential.

But in his jingoistic exuberance Nehemiah had forgotten Ruth, the Moabitess, who had given birth to Obed: "They named him Obed; he was the father of Jesse, the father of David" (Ruth 4:17). From Ruth had come their greatest king, King David, the man the Jews loved, the king who epitomised for them the nobility of their nationhood. So their beloved David was of mixed race, part Moabite, part Jew.

Nearer home
And now turn the pages of your history book to the 1930s, and find yourself in the Germany ruled by Hitler. Hitler's race was to be pure Aryan. Tainted Jewish blood had to be drained away. Jewish blood would contaminate the Teutonic purity. And six million Jews were

exterminated. Hitler's 1930s are a far cry from around the year 1000 BC when Jewish blood, mixed with Moabite blood, brought forth the paragon of the Jews, King David.

It's an interesting parallel. Maybe God is trying to help us of the twenty-first century to get the message from Ezra's and Nehemiah's fifth century.

DAVID

"Why does the king hate me?"
asks David

If I had to choose a friend from the many admirable characters of the Old Testament, my choice would be Jonathan, son of Saul and friend of David.

The name SAUL introduces a new chapter in the history of the Jewish nation. The system of being ruled by Judges had failed miserably. But it was only when the Ark of the Covenant had been captured in battle by the Philistines that the nation got the message: like other victorious nations, Israel needed a king to weld the twelve tribes into a single nation.

By God's order, the prophet Samuel became Israel's first kingmaker when he anointed Saul. In 1025 BC, for the first time in their history, the Jews cried, "God save the king." God tried to. Saul wouldn't let him. Yet Saul, in his early years, had all the qualities of a great leader. "There was not a man among the people of Israel more handsome than he; from his shoulders upward he was taller than any of the people" (1 Samuel 9:2). Jonathan's father started his public life as a national leader. Witness his first act after Samuel consecrated him as the first King of Israel.

The Ammonites defeated the inhabitants of Jabesh-Gilead. Their terms for peace were that they would blind the right eye of every citizen. When Saul heard this his heart burned with rage. He cut up two oxen into tiny pieces and sent a piece round to every part of disunited Israel with the threat: "Whoever does not come out after Saul and Samuel, so shall it be done to his oxen!" (1 Samuel 11:7). The people were in such dread of him that they answered his summons to a man. Needless to say, with such a leader, his 300,000 volunteers slaughtered the Ammonites. Needless to say, with such a leader, the Israelites conquered all their traditional enemies... the Philistines, the Ammonites, the Moabites, the Amalekites and the Syrians. That was the picture of the young King Saul. As he grew older his fine mind crumbled, he was racked with traits of insanity, of melancholy, of arrogance, of intense jealousy leading to violence.

Friends at court

It was jealousy of David that drove an older King Saul to madness and violence. The Philistines had challenged the Israelites to single combat. Their man-at-arms was a giant, Goliath. No Israelite dared fight him. Diminutive David won Saul's permission to champion the Jews. We all learned the outcome when we were in primary school. David killed Goliath with a catapult and a pebble.

Saul was enraged at the sight of the multitude of women who came from all parts of the kingdom to celebrate David's defeat of Goliath. They came singing and dancing merrily with tambour and cymbal. Saul couldn't hear that music. Ringing in his ears, blotting out every other sound, were the words of the women's song: "Saul has slain his thousands, and David his ten thousands" (1 Samuel 18:7).

The next day, as David played his harp for King Saul in the palace, Saul picked up a lance and hurled it at David, hoping to pin him to the wall. Twice this happened and twice David was lucky to escape with his life. David needed friends at court and he found two: Michal, Saul's younger daughter, and Jonathan, Saul's son.

Love at court

Saul was forever scheming to insult David. He had promised his elder daughter, Merab, in marriage to the warrior who conquered Goliath; but when it was David who was victor, Saul craftily postponed the wedding and – to slight David – proceeded to forget his promise and married her off conveniently to Adriel the Meholathite.

Circumstances gave Saul another chance to gloat. He found out that it was not Merab but his younger daughter, Michal, who had won David's affection. Because Saul thought that Michal was as malleable as she was beautiful, he used her as bait to kill David. But that was in vain. Rather, it worked the other way round. When David's life was again threatened, Michal risked her father's wrath and saved David's life by concealing a dummy in his bed and letting David down out of the window. So Michal was friend number one. Jonathan was his second friend and protector.

Jonathan – true friend

Jonathan was a dutiful son, but he would never allow himself to be used against his conscience or his heart. His obedience was for his father, but his affection was for David. He was a fearless warrior. On one occasion, unknown to his father, he crept into the Philistine camp in the night with his armour-bearer and killed twenty soldiers. He, with his two brothers, was by the king's side when the Philistines destroyed the Israelite army at Mount Gilboa. Saul was determined that he would not be taken prisoner: no uncircumcised enemy would be allowed to gloat over the captive king and, having shamed him, kill him. When Saul fell on his own sword, Jonathan already lay dead on the battlefield.

There was empathy between Jonathan and David. In the words of the Bible, "the soul of Jonathan was knit to the soul of David, and Jonathan loved him as his own soul" (1 Samuel 18:1). Saul himself was aware of this. Once in anger he shouted that he had marked how Jonathan loved this son of Jesse: "Therefore send and fetch him to me, for he shall surely die" (1 Samuel 20:31).

The Lord's anointed

In his lifetime it was Jonathan who made all the running because David himself was on the run. David esteemed Saul as God's own representative and was the most faithful of courtiers. Once he actually had Saul's life in his hands. David, to escape Saul's army, set himself up at En-Gedi, a town on the west shore of the Dead Sea. Saul followed him with an army of 3,000 men, although the terrain was so rocky and steep that only the wild goats could find a footing.

Saul needed to ease himself and slipped into a vast cave. In the inner part of that cave David and his men lay hidden. David silently cut off the hem of Saul's cloak. When Saul left the cave, David followed him at a distance and called out, "My lord the king!" (1 Samuel 24:8). Then, showing Saul the hem of the cloak, he said, "Lo, this day your eyes have seen how the Lord gave you today into my hand in the cave; and some bade me kill you, but I spared you. I said, 'I will not put forth my hand against my lord; for he is the Lord's anointed'" (1 Samuel 24:10). Saul cried out, "Is this your voice, my son David?" (1 Samuel 24:16). And Saul wept. It was peace again... till the next bout of insane jealousy.

Time and time again David must have asked Jonathan, "Why does your murderous father hate me? Why ME? I who love and revere the Lord's anointed." Time and time again Jonathan pleaded for David's life in the face of Saul's murderous jealousy. Time and time again he shielded David. Incessantly he risked his own life to save David's life, once risking a spear which was at the ready to transfix David. Jonathan was forever putting David on his guard against Saul, saving his life as he did in the wilderness of Ziph in south Judea, where, in the wooded hills, David and his 600 soldiers had made their home.

Small wonder it was that David broke down when he heard of Jonathan's death at Mount Gilboa, crying out, "your love to me was wonderful, passing the love of women" (2 Samuel 1:26). Jonathan had proved himself to be greater than the rest and better than the best, and well David knew it. We would have had no King David if David had not had his Jonathan.

True friendship
After Jonathan's death it was David's turn to prove his friendship. He set out to find whether there were any descendants of Saul who were in need of help so that he could befriend them for Jonathan's sake. He tracked down Ziba, one of Saul's household, who led him to Jonathan's own son, Mephibosheth. Mephibosheth's nurse had dropped him when he was a baby, breaking both his feet. He was also crippled for life in his spirit. When he was brought to David he said, "What is your servant, that you should look upon a dead dog such as I?" (2 Samuel 9:8).

But he was Jonathan's own son. On him David conferred all the lands that had belonged to Saul, and he gave him faithful Ziba and his fifteen sons and twenty servants to wait on him. Mephibosheth sat at the king's table as though he himself were a king's son. Jonathan would have been proud of David, his friend.

JONAH
Who finally said, "Nineveh, here I come."

At the time of the Assyrian Empire there was a Jewish fellow named Jonah, just going about his business. Always at the back of his mind, like any other Jew of that time, he was suffering from the double pain – oppression and exile. Like any caring Israelite, he nurtured a hatred for all things Assyrian. Assyria, with its capital at Nineveh, had conquered Israel in 721 BC. That conquest rankled and names like King Sennacherib, who had cheated and tricked and destroyed the weaker Israel and driven the vanquished into exile, filled the Israelite mind with loathing.

Over the years Assyria and particularly its capital, Nineveh, had become dens of iniquity. In the Jewish mind there was no difference between Assyria and places like Sodom and Gomorrah or the world of corruption that had led to the Great Flood. Nineveh in particular wallowed in corruption. Even their gods were a wicked and quarrelsome lot, and their temples were the living quarters of harlots – and the hosts of harlots were seldom idle!

It was in this setting that God exploded a bomb. To this ordinary fellow called Jonah God said, "Arise, go to Nineveh, that great city, and cry against it; for their wickedness has come up before me" (Jonah 1:2). This didn't appeal to Jonah one little bit. One can almost hear him saying:

"But WHY ME, LORD?"

God did not hear Jonah say it because Jonah was no longer there to argue with God! He decided to disappear. He found a ship going to Tarshish (today, Sardinia). He paid his fare and went aboard. God would look for him in vain.

Puffed up with pride

Preachers usually depict Jonah as a coward. He was no coward, but he was a very proud man. Jonah was also a man of great faith. He understood God's qualities, particularly his love and mercy. What Jonah dreaded was that his preaching to the Ninevites would convert them. His loathing for all people and things Assyrian was deeply imbedded in him. Well he knew that if the Ninevites repented an all-merciful God would forgive them. And Jonah would far rather see God punish them as he had punished Sodom and Gomorrah. His joy would have been to stay at a distance and gleefully watch the Ninevites burn to the last man, woman, child and beast.

But here, for Jonah, was the rub. He was acting as a prophet. He had prophesied that Nineveh would be destroyed. But here was Jonah's fear. The Ninevites might repent and then God would forgive their wrongdoing; and Jonah would lose face. So, to make sure this proud man wouldn't lose face, he ran away from God.

But Jonah did lose face
Shortly after the start of the journey there came a mighty storm, so strong that the ship was on the point of sinking. Jonah slept. He was awakened and had to explain that he was running away from the Lord. As the storm continued with unabated fury the sailors cast lots as to who had brought this storm on. The lot fell on Jonah, and Jonah – at his own suggestion – was thrown overboard and the storm subsided.

The Bible puts the sequel so neatly: "And the Lord appointed a great fish to swallow up Jonah; and Jonah was in the belly of the fish three days and three nights" (Jonah 1:17). "And the Lord spoke to the fish, and it vomited out Jonah upon the dry land" (Jonah 2:10).

Nineveh at last
Again God ordered Jonah to go to Nineveh and Jonah this time obeyed. He proclaimed to the Ninevites that after forty days Nineveh was going to be destroyed. The people, from the king downwards, believed him. They also believed that the Israelite God was a merciful God. The nation pleaded and fasted in sackcloth and ashes, and God relented and did not inflict the proclaimed punishment on them.

Mercies multiplied

During these penitential forty days Jonah had been waiting for the disaster. But the disaster never happened. And Jonah, wounded in his pride, fell into a rage, begging God to let him die, to which God replied by asking whether he, Jonah, had the right to be angry. And then God set out to answer the question himself.

While he waited for the catastrophe Jonah had made himself a shelter so as to witness the tragedy which was to hit Nineveh. Then God arranged that a castor oil plant should grow over him to shade him from the heat of the sun. Jonah was thrilled. But at dawn next day a worm attacked the plant and it withered and the sun beat down mercilessly on Jonah's head. Jonah was livid and complained to God.

God's answer lives in the history of humanity. He reproached Jonah: "You pity the plant, for which you did not labour, nor did you make it grow, which came into being in a night, and perished in a night. And should not I pity Nineveh, that great city, in which there are more than a hundred and twenty thousand persons who do not know their right hand from their left, and also much cattle?" (Jonah 4:10-11).

Could God give Jonah – and our own selves – a more striking proof of his mercy, his forgiveness and his love?

NAAMAN
A triple "Why me?"

One of the great characters of the Bible must surely be the little girl whose name we don't know, who was created to pronounce one sentence, and then to return to the oblivion from which she came. Unknown to herself, she gave the total answer to a question which, at some time, worries and perplexes almost every person of every century. The question is:

"WHY ME?"

The little Jewess was a slave. She had been captured by Syrian freebooters in one of their frequent raids against the Jews. She must have been a beautiful and intelligent child because it was none other than the commander of the Syrian army, called Naaman, who bought her. She was a slave in an enviable household where husband and wife were very much united in love. Naaman himself must have been a model of courtesy: it was on his arm that the aged King Benhadad leaned when he made his way to the temple to pay homage to his gods.

That Naaman was a good and kind man would have given little consolation to the little slave. It didn't make sense. Out of the thousands of youngsters the Syrians could have captured, it had to be herself.

"Why ME?"

she must have asked herself as she sobbed herself to sleep.

That Naaman was a good and kind man would have given little consolation to the child's parents. It takes little imagination to hear their question which confuses most of us at times: "Why did God do this to US?" They would treasure the child's belongings in their love for her, doubting as they did so the love of God for them.

"Why OUR child?"

they would repeatedly say as they sobbed themselves to sleep.

The leper

Naaman was an outstanding man in the kingdom, but his jewelled turban and silken robe hid his tragedy: he had become a leper. His was a white leprosy which in those days was incurable. Time and time again he must have asked himself, "Why did the gods do this to me?"

"Why ME?"

He loved his gods. The question why they had deserted him must have obsessed him as he gave his arm to his enfeebled king, as they went to the temple to worship Rimmon. He was the kind of man who deserved better.

One tiny sentence

It was that very leprosy which was to lead Naaman from his gods to God, and the little Jewish girl was destined to guide him. Ingenuously she uttered to her mistress the sentence around which God had shaped her life: "Would that my lord were with the prophet who is in Samaria! He would cure him of his leprosy" (2 Kings 5:3).

Her mission was ended. She had uttered the sentence which it was her predestined role to utter. And she disappeared into history, little knowing that she had changed history.

The healing Jordan waters

The remainder of the story is well known: how the Syrian commander went to Elisha; how, on the prophet's instructions, he bathed seven times in the River Jordan; how his flesh healed up and became like the flesh of a little child; and how, in finding health, he found God: "Behold, I know that there is no God in all the earth but in Israel" (2 Kings 5:15).

Naaman's conversion gives one further insight into his character, and into the totality of his gift of himself to the Lord. He had a scruple. He put it to Elisha. His was the privilege of helping his frail king to the temple to worship what he now knew as a false god. He could not fail his king. He felt it his duty to continue to help him, and this meant assisting him to the temple of the false gods. So thorough was his own conversion that he had to clear with Elisha that the Lord would understand his motive and forgive him.

Peace

But the little slave girl had a still greater mission than the healing of the Syrian commander. This was a means to a greater end for Israel. Syria was the most feared neighbour of the Jews because it was the most covetous. There was perpetual war, with Syria usually the aggressor. The healing of the body and soul of Naaman was to change all that. Naaman, says the Bible, was high in his master's favour. They walked and talked together; they prayed together. His was the counsel the king would follow.

Elisha refused the Syrian king's proffered payment for the cure – ten talents of silver, 6,000 gold pieces and ten suits of clothes. But Naaman asked Elisha for an extraordinary gift for his own self: "If not, I pray you, let there be given to your servant two mules' burden of earth; for henceforth your servant will not offer burnt offering or sacrifice to any god but the Lord" (2 Kings 5:17).

Is it likely that the commander who begged two mules' worth of Israel's soil would order his armies to go into the attack and take all the land of Israel? An unknown little slave girl's one sentence gave healing to Naaman and peace to Israel.

Faithful to her faith

There's one point in the story which might well be overlooked. Judah and Israel produced some great women: Deborah who conquered five Canaanite armies, Judith who conquered Holofernes, Esther who saved her nation from total annihilation. Israel also produced one little slave girl who was equally great: she conquered herself. She was so young when she was taken captive. She had so little time to grasp all the teachings of her Jewish faith. Yet her faith was of the finest.

She lived in a household which worshipped its own gods. She was surrounded by Baals and Molochs and Rimmons, all-pervading and often all-degrading, with their devious priests and their temple prostitutes. The pagan atmosphere in which she lived ran counter to all that her own God had taught. Others deserted their God and worshipped pagan gods in high places, where the children of Israel followed the nations that were around them and "forsook all the commandments of the Lord their God, and made for themselves molten images of two calves... and worshipped all the host of heaven, and served Baal" (2 Kings 17:16).

Not so our young Jewess of Naaman's household. In that pagan setting, all alone, she remained firm in her faith, true to her God. And that was no small conquest!

JEREMIAH
"Why me, oh God, why me?"
groans Jeremiah

If ever there was a man who could rightly say, "Why ME?" that man was Jeremiah. Rembrandt, in his portrait of Jeremiah, caught the very mood of the man: brooding, melancholic, introspective. Michelangelo created the same tragic figure on the ceiling of the Sistine Chapel where Jeremiah sits, a giant of a man, slumped with hands on chin, with lacklustre eyes pondering a frightening future.

But this was not the youthful Jeremiah. Young Jeremiah was a country yokel whose joy was to see the almond trees in full bloom in his native village of Anathoth, a few miles north of Jerusalem. But God called him out of his serene, rural retreat and, with that call, Jeremiah stepped into a life of unremitting hatred, bitterness, persecution... When he left his almond blossoms he had only one consolation; and that was that he carried through with the work he hated because that was the work that God called him to do.

God calls

From the first, Jeremiah feared God's call. When, 100 years earlier, Isaiah had heard God ask, "Whom shall I send, and who will go for us?" Isaiah had promptly answered, "Here am I! Send me" (Isaiah 6:8). And God sent one of the seraphim who touched Isaiah's lips with a burning coal, making them, as it were, God's lips for God's work.

When, 100 years later, God called Jeremiah for similar work, Jeremiah tried to wriggle out of his vocation with a plea similar to that which Moses had used before him. "Why me, Lord?" he must have asked as he pleaded, "Behold, I do not know how to speak, for I am only a youth" (Jeremiah 1:6). Jeremiah had, indeed, just passed the teenage stage of life. But, as with Moses, God would brook no refusal. He affirmed, "Before I formed you in the womb I knew you, and before you were born I consecrated you; I appointed you a prophet to the nations" (Jeremiah 1:5). And God touched the reluctant Jeremiah's lips, and they became – so to speak – God's lips.

Then God spelt out Jeremiah's vocation: "See, I have set you this day over nations and over kingdoms, to pluck up and to break down, to destroy and to overthrow, to build and to plant" (Jeremiah 1:10). What a task for a yokel who loved to recline among the almond trees, and to catch the delicate pink and white petals as they floated through the air.

A lifelong mission

His lifelong work was to bring his own people back to God. Israel had forgotten the God who had brought them out of Egypt. They had turned to false gods. "And I will utter my judgments against them, for all their wickedness in forsaking me; they have burned incense to other gods, and worshipped the works of their own hands" (Jeremiah 1:16). That was God's summing-up of his chosen people, and that was the message that Jeremiah had to proclaim in God's name.

Further, the whole moral framework had collapsed. Israel seemed to have exceeded the wickedness of Sodom and Gomorrah. When Abraham pleaded for the inhabitants of Sodom and Gomorrah he was assured that the cities would be saved if he found ten just men. And fire consumed the cities.

Jeremiah was assured that Jerusalem would be saved if he found just one just man! "Run to and fro through the streets of Jerusalem, look and take note! Search her squares to see if you can find a man, one who does justice and seeks truth; that I may pardon her" (Jeremiah 5:1). And Jerusalem was razed to the ground!

Day in, day out, in the streets, at the Temple gate, for forty years, Jeremiah had to reproach the very people he lived with. His mission was to petition, to cajole, to warn, to threaten them in their blind obstinacy, for their rejection of their God.

Voice in the wilderness

Jeremiah was a powerful speaker with an exceptional flair for getting his message across. He was what they would call today a past master in the use of visual aids to give dramatic impact to his words. Even the least intelligent could not fail to get his message. Denouncing the wickedness of the Israelites, he buried his clothes. Then he dug them up and told the gaping crowd that their faith was like that: once it was white and clean. Today it is buried, mouldy, maggoty. Another time he took a clay pot and shattered it to show what God was going to do to the nation if they did not repent. To stress a message he hated to give – of submission to the Babylonians – he carried a yoke around his neck to show the Israelites their fate if they went it alone and counted on the protection of Egypt.

Jeremiah had to spell out the fate of the Israelites if they did not repent. If they continued to reject their God, their God would reject them: "I will make Jerusalem a heap of ruins, a lair of jackals; and I will make the cities of Judah a desolation, without inhabitant" (Jeremiah 9:11). These things Jeremiah hated to say. These things the people hated to hear, and they hated Jeremiah for saying them.

The crunch came when scorn and loathing so overwhelmed him that Jeremiah could take no more. In his anguish he cried, "Cursed be the day on which I was born! The day when my mother bore me, let it not be blessed!... Why did I come forth from the womb to see toil and sorrow, and spend my days in shame?" (Jeremiah 20:14, 18).

"I have become a laughingstock all the day; every one mocks me. For whenever I speak, I cry out, I shout, 'Violence and destruction!' For the word of the Lord has become for me a reproach and derision all day long" (Jeremiah 20:7-8). But God didn't let him escape. "If I say, 'I will not mention him, or speak any more in his name,' there is in my heart as it were a burning fire shut up in my bones, and I am weary with holding it in, and I cannot" (Jeremiah 20:9).

The strident voice of Jeremiah's reproaches continued to echo through the marketplace to the very throne room of the palace. He wrote on a scroll all God's warnings, and Baruch, his secretary, read them out to the king. Before the scroll was finished, King Jehoiakim took his penknife and began cutting the scroll in pieces, which he threw on the brazier of lighted coals till the whole book had perished in the flames. So much for repentance!

The political scene

Jeremiah's role carried him into the political sea, and he had to swim against the political tide. Babylon threatened their country, and the Jewish leaders looked to Egypt for salvation. Jeremiah had to issue God's decree: king and people were to submit to Babylon. Babylon should not be resisted and Israel should accept the total loss of its land and the exile of its people.

Again and again Jeremiah had to threaten his own people, and this Jeremiah hated to do. And his threats were devastating: to remain in Jerusalem meant death by sword, famine and pestilence. Only by going over, not to the Egyptians but to the Chaldeans, would they be saved. This was blasphemy, defeatism and treason. The anger these words inspired inflamed the people to violence. Jeremiah walked in fear of his life. Twice his death was plotted. He was put in the stocks. He was left to die in a dried-up well. When politicians fled from the Babylonians into Egypt, Jeremiah was dragged with them. From that moment we lose sight of him.

Peace in pain

From the day when he was called from the peace of his almond trees, Jeremiah had not one year, not one day of peace. He ranks among the most hated men of the world. Yet however much he himself hated his vocation to upbraid his own countrymen, he never swerved from the path on which God had planted his feet. His was among the saddest, the most tragic missions ever given by God to man.

But among all this brooding desolation he did have one consolation: that was that he had kept faith with man because he had kept faith with God. His deepest joy was that nearly all God's threats ended on a note of hope: "Go, and proclaim these words toward the north, and say, 'Return, faithless Israel, says the Lord. I will not look on you in anger, for I am merciful, says the Lord; I will not be angry for ever'" (Jeremiah 3:12).

Jeremiah knew that a loving God would destroy a nation only to build a better nation – and that from that renewed nation the Messiah would come. Because he, Jeremiah, understood and believed this message, his own heart, in the midst of torments, was at peace.

J O B
Who saw beyond the "Why me?"

This is a most intriguing story of a contest between God and Satan. It all centred around a holy man called Job, living in the middle of the fifth century before Christ.

God was so proud of Job. Job was righteous, he was God-fearing, and his whole life centred around his family – he was a model parent – and the Lord. Job was so proud of God. God had blessed him with all that a man could materially desire. God had given love for love... and an abundance of good things besides.

God, in his graciousness, had given Job seven sons and three daughters; and they were a lovely set. They enjoyed a round of jolly parties with rollicking companions, and Job smiled benignly on their frolics. When their week of feasting was over, Job would send for them, and next morning would offer a burnt offering for each of them. He mused, "It may be that my sons have sinned, and cursed God in their hearts" (Job 1:5). He wanted to keep them close to the Lord. They were going to be rich when their father died because God had made him a wealthy man. He owned 7,000 sheep, 3,000 camels, 500 yoke of oxen and 500 she-asses. Indeed, Job was at peace with God, and well he might be!

Confrontation
And now the stage is set for the drama.

Act One
God meets Satan, who had been roaming to and fro about the earth. God asks, "Have you considered my servant Job, that there is none like him on the earth, a blameless and upright man, who fears God and turns away from evil?" (Job 1:8).

The devil sneers, "Does Job fear God for nought? Hast thou not put a hedge about him and his house and all that he has, on every side? Thou hast blessed the work of his hands, and his possessions have increased in the land. But put forth thy hand now, and touch all that he has, and he will curse thee to thy face" (Job 1:9-11).

God smiled a knowing smile, and in full confidence gave Satan permission to ruin Job, but without physically harming him. He'd teach Satan a thing or two!

To have a go at Job was just the job for Satan. Satan knew – and told God so – that Job's devotion was only skin deep, and that disaster would transform piety into impiety, prayers into curses, and blessings into blasphemy.

Act Two
Satan wasted no time. He'd teach God a thing or two. Blow after grievous blow the devil struck.

A messenger arrives panting and blurts out that Job's oxen have been stolen by the Sabeans and his servants slain; he alone was alive to tell the tale. Following on this messenger came another: lightning had killed sheep and shepherds; he alone was alive to tell the tale. A third arrived to tell how the Chaldeans had driven away Job's 3,000 camels and slain his men; he alone was alive to tell the tale.

The greatest tragedy was still to come. All Job's sons and daughters were feasting. A tempestuous wind blew down the house, crushing all his ten children. And the malicious devil stood by smirking, waiting for the curses. And well he might. But the curses never came.

Act Three
What Satan saw, Satan didn't like. Job didn't raise clenched fists and scream curses at God. He didn't even query, "Why has God done this to ME? WHY ME?" To the devil's chagrin, Job bowed down to earth and did reverence to God, saying words which have echoed down the centuries: "The Lord gave, and the Lord has taken away; blessed be the name of the Lord" (Job 1:21).

And God declared triumphantly to Satan that Job had still not denied him.

Act Four – Satan's last throw

The devil had the answer to that: "Skin for skin! All that a man has he will give for his life. But put forth thy hand now, and touch his bone and his flesh, and he will curse thee to thy face" (Job 2:4-5).

So God gave Satan permission to afflict Job's body, and Satan smote Job with a foul scab from head to foot, so that he had to sit down on the dunghill and scratch himself with a shard where he itched.

Now these were the days when people thought that pain was God's punishment for sin... usually secret sins. It was in this mood that his wife attacked him: "Do you still hold fast your integrity? Curse God, and die" (Job 2:9). Next it was three friends that came to console Job: Eliphaz, Bildad and Zophar. Console? They chided him insistently for sinning in secret: hence God's punishment. A fourth "friend", Elihu, joined the accusing trio. Elihu was a bombastic, conceited, self-important fellow, top-heavy with accusations. And they didn't lose in the telling! Poor, suffering Job! They would have done better by bringing a first-aid kit, bandaging his wounds and anointing his sores.

Strength in weakness

Even heroes have their weaknesses. His sufferings and the constant reproaches of his "friends" broke Job and he cursed, not God, but the day when he was born. "Why me?" must have been the horrendous cry which his agony forced from him.

But it was a temporary weakness. He recovered his faith in God and he made a confession of faith which must rank among the greatest acts of faith in the Bible:

"For I know that my Redeemer lives,
and at last he will stand upon the earth;
and after my skin has been thus destroyed,
then from my flesh I shall see God..." (Job 19:25-26).

(Stage directions)

Enter a smiling God and exit a snarling Satan, to music of an angelic choir singing Job's act of faith, which Handel put to music in *The Messiah* about 2,200 years later.

Final Act

At such faith, God's heart was moved. Had trust in God, blind, believing trust, ever been surpassed in the history of the human race?

"And the Lord blessed the latter days of Job more than his beginning; and he had fourteen thousand sheep, six thousand camels, a thousand yoke of oxen, and a thousand she-asses. He had also seven sons and three daughters... And in all the land there were no women so fair as Job's daughters..." (Job 42:12-15).

> Is the story of Job a fact? Was there such a man?
> Is the story of Job a parable?
> Does it matter?
> The message is eternal.

ESTHER
The queen who fearfully asks,
"Why me?"

Helena Rubenstein is reported to have said that with all her art she could never match the serenity of a nun's face. Yet the creative beauty in which Helena excels once saved the whole Jewish race.

It was around twenty-four centuries ago when the Persians had defeated the Babylonians. The ruler of the civilised world in those days was Ahasuerus of Persia. His rule extended from India, to Ethiopia, to the Persian Gulf. To celebrate the third year of his reign he gave a great feast to all his 127 vassal kings, his governors and his warriors.

They kept riotous holiday for 180 days, and banqueted for the last seven days. The king and guests reclined on golden and silver couches, and they drank from golden goblets. The king's queen, Vashti, held a similar banquet for royal and noble wives. On the seventh day the king was merry and warmed by the long draughts of wine. He decided to blind his guests with the sheer beauty of his queen. He sent seven chamberlains to bring the crowned Queen Vasthi into his presence.

A royal refusal

Stupefaction. Rage. The queen refused to be exhibited to a drunken rabble, no matter how apparently royal they were. The king appealed to his wise councillors to suggest a punishment. One, Prince Memucan, went straight to the point: "Not only to the king has Queen Vashti done wrong, but also to all the princes and all the peoples who are in all the provinces of King Ahasuerus. For this deed of the queen will be made known to all women, causing them to look with contempt upon their husbands, since they will say, 'King Ahasuerus commanded Queen Vashti to be brought before him, and she did not come'" (Esther 1:16-17). And immediately that noble, intoxicated assembly, standing in as both judge and jury, endorsed the sentence. In his fury Ahasuerus banished Queen Vashti from his court and sent couriers throughout the empire to find the most beautiful virgins, one of whom was to take the place of the disgraced queen.

The beautician's salon

These damsels were to be committed to the care of chamberlain Hegai, who was to spare no expense in adding cosmetic art to natural beauty. Hegai's sensitivity had the world's gardens to draw on. In the Book of Exodus it is mentioned that Moses ordered perfume from fragrant cinnamon, liquid myrrh, cassia, senna and olive oil to anoint the Ark of the Covenant. To anoint the Tent of Meeting there had to be a mixture of storax, onycha, galbanum and frankincense. These cosmetics were so precious that they could not be traded for profane use.

Each nation also produced its substances to be textured into fragrance. From Egypt came myrrh, from China musk with hyacinth, almonds and calamus. Cleopatra, at a later date, bettered the expertise of former generations, acquired Jericho and turned the plain into a garden of aromatic spices which ensnared Julius Caesar and Mark Antony, and nearly captivated Herod the Great.

A chamberlain bewitched

Living beside the palace of Ahasuerus was a Jew called Mordecai who had been brought there into captivity by Nebuchadnezzar. He was a Benjaminite, descended from King Saul. He cherished his ward, an orphan, who was not only named after the goddess Ishtar, but also had the bearings of a goddess. He kept his own and Esther's nationality a secret, and managed to get Esther accepted among the maidens who were potential occupiers of the queen's throne. Hegai was bewitched by her charm, and form and face, and placed her in the care of seven of his most skilful maids of the palace. They served her with the choicest foods and Hegai lavished all his and his maids' skills on her.

Each queenly candidate had to be prepared for twelve months before being presented to the king. For six months each one was anointed with oils, and for six months with paints and powders. On the testing day she had unlimited choice of the finest garments, and then she was presented to the king for his favour, his throne or his harem.

Finally it was Esther's turn to be assessed by the king. This demi-goddess had beauty beyond belief to win men's favours and their love. The king himself succumbed immediately to her charms, set the crown on her head and, without delay, proclaimed a bridal feast and a public holiday throughout all his dominions.

Lusting for power

A certain Haman, prime minister to Ahasuerus, lusted for power, and – vain man – he gave an order that, whenever he passed, everyone should bow the knee and do him reverence. Mordecai, scion of kings, was of an independent breed and refused to bend so low. Haman's anger turned into an obsession of hatred, first with the man, and then, when he learned that Mordecai was a Jew, with the whole Jewish race. He engineered that the king should sign a decree ordering that on the 13th of the month Adar (which corresponds to February or early March in our calendar), every Jew throughout the empire was to be exterminated.

Esther, saviour

This news reached Mordecai. When the decree was signed, but before the date of execution, Mordecai begged the queen to plead with the king for their own people.

"Why ME?"

must have been the spontaneous reaction of Esther. And then came proof that beauty can be more than skin deep. Esther was as brave as she was beautiful, and she was very beautiful.

In that autocratic age, to appear in the inner court without a royal summons was courting death, and Ahasuerus was a man of many moods. When, for instance, a storm broke a bridge of boats which his soldiers had manoeuvred into position across the Hellespont when he was invading Greece, he ordered the waves to be scourged with 300 lashes.

Esther knew that the king's sceptre had the power of life or death. She was also aware that she had not been summoned to the king's presence for thirty days. She put her trust in God. She sent word to Mordecai, asking him to get the people to fast and pray for three days. Then she added words of incomparable courage: "I and my maids will also fast as you do. Then I will go to the king, though it is against the law; and if I perish, I perish" (Esther 4:16).

On the third day Esther put on her royal robes and stood at the door of the throne room. Ahasuerus saw her. The courtiers saw her. There must have been a dramatic hush: a hush of life or death. Mercifully, the golden sceptre beckoned her in. With relief bordering on total collapse, she kissed the tip of the royal rod. "What is your petition, Queen Esther? It shall be granted you. And what is your request? Even to the half of my kingdom, it shall be fulfilled" (Esther 7:2).

Esther was saved. Her nation was saved. Had she died, as well she might, there would have been no Jewish nation. A woman, as brave as she was beautiful, gave us the Messiah.

The 14th of Adar

Never has the Jewish nation forgotten Esther's heroism which saved them from annihilation throughout the Persian Empire. In every synagogue throughout the world on the evening before the 14th of Adar and again in the morning of the 14th of Adar, the Esther story is read. The 14th of Adar, the feast of Purim, is a public holiday throughout the Jewish world. Gifts are exchanged among friends and alms are given to the poor so that everyone will delight in joyful festivities.

In the synagogue of Nazareth and in his home, Our Lord each year would have been enthralled by the story of Esther. How well he who later was to agonise over the fear of death in Gethsemane would have understood Esther's fear of death as she stood at the entrance to the throne room of Ahasuerus. "Father, if thou art willing, remove this cup from me; nevertheless not my will, but thine, be done" (Luke 22:42). Would Our Lord have thought of Esther when he said, "Greater love has no man than this, that a man lay down his life for his friends"? (John 15:13).

JOHN THE BAPTIST
Zechariah and Elizabeth knew the answer

To find the most idyllic scene in the Bible, one could well go to a tiny hamlet lost in the rolling hills and verdant valleys of Judea, a few miles from Jerusalem – a tiny village called En Karem. In this hamlet, at the time of Herod the Great, a great drama was to unfold, the impact of which was to go beyond En Karem to the very end of the earth and to the end of time.

An ageing couple lived there in total contentment except for one disappointment. The ageing couple were Zechariah and Elizabeth. Zechariah was a priest, taking his turn at the Temple altar duties, and Elizabeth was from the House of Aaron. St Luke metes out high praise to this couple: "And they were both righteous before God, walking in all the commandments and ordinances of the Lord blameless" (Luke 1:6).

They were ageing graciously and gracefully, with only one sorrow. Elizabeth was barren. For most married women, infertility is a bitter blow. For an Israelite woman it was a double blow, because it was from some Israelite woman that the Messiah was to come.

"Would that I could..."
"If only...", Elizabeth would sigh as she tossed on a sleepless pillow. How much she must have envied the wife of Manoah of Dan who was barren. To Manoah's wife an angel had appeared and said, "Behold, you are barren and have no children; but you shall conceive and bear a son... and he shall begin to deliver Israel from the hand of the Philistines" (Judges 13:3-5). And that son was the great Samson.

How much she must have envied Elkanah's wife, Hannah, who was also barren, who would sit in the Temple in tears, with no heart for eating. God, in answer to Hannah's and the High Priest's prayers, gave her a son. And that son was Samuel, Israel's man of destiny. But alas, Elizabeth and Zechariah knew that she herself was well past the age when such a dream could come true.

Drama!

One day Zechariah and Elizabeth were delirious with delight. A great honour had come to their home. Zechariah's name had been drawn by lot to carry the fire from the outer altar of burning to the golden altar of incense in the inner sanctuary of the Temple, while the whole multitude of the people stood praying outside at the hour of sacrifice.

As he approached the altar, Zechariah saw an angel standing to the right of the altar. It was the Archangel Gabriel. Gabriel announced that Elizabeth was to become the mother of a son. "And you will have joy and gladness, and many will rejoice at his birth," Gabriel said, "for he will be great before the Lord, and he shall drink no wine nor strong drink, and he will be filled with the Holy Spirit, even from his mother's womb. And he will turn many of the sons of Israel to the Lord their God, and he will go before him in the spirit and power of Elijah, to turn the hearts of the fathers to the children, and the disobedient to the wisdom of the just, to make ready for the Lord a people prepared" (Luke 1:14-17).

There is an expression: "to be struck dumb" – lost in amazement. For Zechariah this was doubly true. He was indeed lost in amazement. He also doubted the archangel's message, and Gabriel said, "And behold, you will be silent and unable to speak until the day that these things come to pass, because you did not believe my words, which will be fulfilled in their time" (Luke 1:20).

"Here John was born"

At En Karem there are twin churches. Over the home where John was born an admiring Church has built a church, and on the floor of this rock home which the church covers is a circle with five crosses and the words: "Here John was born." John, Our Lord's cousin, blessed in his birth, was hounded in his infancy and hounded in his death; but, in between, was a span of life so magnificent that Our Lord said of him, "I tell you, among those born of women none is greater than John..." (Luke 7:28).

A second church is hidden in the hillside. The story runs – and it seems a most probable story – that Herod heard of the birth of a wonder-child at En Karem... a miracle birth to an aged mother, a miracle birth at which the dumb spoke. Echoes of this wonder would have reached Jerusalem very fast. The Temple would have been buzzing with the news of John's birth as it had buzzed nine months before: "What then will this child be?" (Luke 1:66).

Because Zechariah was so strongly linked with the Temple, and because En Karem is only five miles from Jerusalem, it would have been strange if Herod's minions did not catch up with the news. It would have been strange if Herod had not sent soldiers to En Karem, as he had sent soldiers to Bethlehem, to seek and slay the child. In the hills above the village was a spring in a cave. To that cave, the story goes, Elizabeth took the child until the furore was over. The doomed child was safe. Around that cave and spring stands one of the most beautiful churches in the Holy Land.

Infatuation

Lucky in his birth, John was not so lucky in his death. Herod Antipas was one of the sons of Herod the Great. The latter was the Herod at the time of the birth of Our Lord. At his death he divided his empire among three sons, and one of them, Herod Antipas, became Tetrarch of Galilee. He was Tetrarch for forty-three years, and so he was "Herod the Fox" whose name is linked with Pontius Pilate and the crucifixion. He built up Tiberias, with its medicinal springs on the shore of the Sea of Galilee, as his capital.

On a visit to Rome he linked up with his half-brother, Herod Philip. It would be fairer to say that he linked up with his half-brother's wife, Herodias. She was married to Herod Philip and lived in Rome. She had a daughter of great charm, Salome. But they were living private lives in Rome, whereas Herod Antipas was a power in Galilee and Peraea.

Who enticed whom we shall never know. What we do know is that Herod Antipas married Herodias and that their marriage was a double fault. Herod Antipas divorced his own wife to marry Herodias, his half-brother's wife: that was the first fault. The marriage was incestuous because he married the wife of his own half-brother: that made it a double fault.

John the Baptist's condemnation of Herod had its searing echo in the mind of Herodias. The cry had to be silenced: only thus would she find peace. She engineered John's death and a besotted Herod gave Salome of the Seven Veils the head of John the Baptist on a dish to give to her mother.

A magnetic character

Between his birth and his death, John stands as a model for all people.

John's was a full life. Guide books like to place him among the pure and penitential Essenes in their Qumran monastery in the Judean desert beside the Dead Sea. It is here that he might well have stayed as he prepared himself in prayer for his public witness of Christ. This is, however, pure conjecture. There is no evidence to substantiate it. If his was a life of prayer, it was also a life of penance. There is little comfort in a desert, and little possibility of gastronomical indulgence in a diet of locusts and wild honey. His was a magnetic character. His preaching attracted large crowds to him, and he held them enthralled by his presence and his preaching.

In his preaching he pulled no punches. To the multitudes who asked what they should do he said, "He who has two coats, let him share with him who has none; and he who has food, let him do likewise" (Luke 3:11). To the tax collectors he preached, "Collect no more than is appointed you" (Luke 3:13). To soldiers who asked for guidance he said firmly, "Rob no one by violence or by false accusation, and be content with your wages" (Luke 3:14).

In spite of John's rough appearance in clothes of camel's hair, charisma and empathy must have radiated from him. This is proved by the school of disciples who grouped themselves around him. Public applause never went to his head. He was too humble for that. He withdrew into the wings to let Christ take the centre of the stage. To his followers he must have asked:

"Why ME?"

And, pointing to Christ, he told them, "He must increase, but I must decrease" (John 3:30). Christ is the star: John is merely the stage hand. John's loss of followers was – as he wanted it to be – Christ's gain. He himself was not worthy to untie the straps of Christ's sandals.

John shared Our Lord's hatred of hypocrisy. Christ called the Pharisees and Sadducees whitened sepulchres – beautiful without, corrupt within. John did not mince his own words either: they were a brood of vipers. He was bold enough to confront the king: "It is not lawful for you to have your brother's wife" (Mark 6:18). He paid for his forthrightness with his life.

The colossus

John bestrides the Old and the New Testaments. In the Old he pleads: "Prepare the way of the Lord, make his paths straight" (Luke 3:4). In the New he looks ahead: "Behold, the Lamb of God, who takes away the sin of the world!" (John 1:29).

His life is so finely attuned to God that when, as he baptised Christ, a voice from heaven said, "Thou art my beloved Son" (Luke 3:22), we can be sure that the Father was also embracing John.

Why ME?...